# MINIFIGURE
## ULTIMATE STICKER COLLECTION

## How to use this book

Read the captions in the 31-page booklet, then turn
to the sticker pages and choose the picture that best
fits in the space available.

•

Don't forget that your stickers can be stuck down and
peeled off again. If you are careful, you can even use
your stickers more than once.

•

You can also use the stickers to decorate your own
books or belongings.

LONDON, NEW YORK, MUNICH,
MELBOURNE, AND DELHI

Written and edited by Victoria Taylor
Designed by Julie Thompson
Jacket designed by Lisa Lanzarini

First American Edition, 2010
10 11 12 13 14 10 9 8 7 6 5
LD109—04/10

Published in the United States by
DK Publishing
375 Hudson Street
New York, New York 10014

ISBN: 978-0-7566-5984-4

Reproduced by Alta Image, London
Printed and bound by L-Rex Printing Co., Ltd, China

Discover more at
www.dk.com
www.LEGO.com

# LEGO® CITY

There is a fire in LEGO® City! Fire fighters rush to the scene with their fire truck. The powerful hoses shoot water over the flames to put out the fire. Many people look on as the men get to work saving lives.

## Police Officer

There is not much crime in LEGO City, but the Police are always on hand to uphold LEGO City laws and to stop any criminals in their tracks.

## Construction Worker

Builders work hard to make sure the people of LEGO City have all the things they need. They build everything from homes to new roads.

## Worker

People work in the many offices in LEGO City. They have to wear smart suits to work.

## Airplane Controller

There is a lot to see in LEGO City. The airport is always busy with tourists so airplanes need to be directed.

## Pilot

This pilot works for the Fire Service. He flies a helicopter over large fires to hose them down from the air.

## Coast Guards

The weather can quickly change on the Coast of LEGO City, but the Coastguards are always on call to bring troubled crew to safety in their helicopter.

## Medical Care

If the citizens of LEGO City feel unwell, they can always rely on the doctor to get them back on their feet.

## Fire Fighter

Fire Fighters are fully trained and are prepared to put out fires and rescue cats from trees!

FIRE

# LEGO® TRAIN

The rail station in LEGO® City is a very busy place. Many people use the railway every day to travel to other cities. Lots of people also work here, including train drivers, engineers, conductors, and track builders.

## Engineer Max

The train driver takes passengers to many other towns and cities. Sometimes he waves to the men working on the track.

## Passenger

Every passenger must buy a ticket before they board the train.

## Railway Engineer

This railway engineer makes sure the trains and tracks are in good condition.

## Railway Employee

This railway worker wears a hard hat and brightly-colored clothing to keep him safe on the rails.

## Passenger

This lady is traveling to work. She carries a briefcase with her, which contains lots of important documents.

## Passenger Train Engineer

The engineer makes sure everything runs to timetable at the LEGO City rail station.

## Railway Employee

The station must be kept clean and tidy at all times. This worker is sweeping the platform.

## Conductor Charlie

The conductor checks that every passenger has a ticket. He wears a smart uniform and a black hat.

# LEGO® CASTLE

A LEGO® castle is under attack! Warriors have to defend their castles from their enemies. They arm themselves with axes and bows and arrows to stop people from other kingdoms from invading.

## Crown King

The Crown King is ruler of his kingdom and leader of the Crown Knights who help him to defend his castle.

## Crown Knight

The crown knights are members of the King's army. They defend the King's castle from trolls, skeletons, and fierce dragons.

## Good Wizard

The Good Wizard wears a hat with stars on and sometimes wears a cape with a lightening bolt on. His greatest enemy is the Evil Wizard.

## Crown Princess

The princess is the daughter of King Leo and Queen Leonora.

## Troll Warrior Orc

The troll warriors help the Evil Wizard to attack the Crown King's castle and the Crown Knights.

## Giant Troll

The Giant Troll has silver horns and wears heavy armor. He carries drumsticks to protect himself.

## Evil Wizard
The Evil Wizard lives in Skelton Tower. He is also ruler of an army of skeletons who help him to defend his castle.

## Black Skeleton
The black knight skeleton will do anything to capture the castle! He leads the evil wizard's army across the kingdom.

# LEGO® PIRATES

The pirates sail the seven seas looking for treasure. The seas are rough and the treasure chest is buried deep. The Navy's soldiers want to get to the treasure first, but the pirates have maps. Who will win?

## Castaway

This castaway has been stranded on a desert island. He has a telescope to look out for passing ships.

## Captain Brickbeard

Captain Brickbeard's outfit is very grand. He has gold buttons and gold epaulets. He is nearly as shiny as the treasure!

## Pirate

Pirates need to protect themselves and their treasure so they often carry swords.

## Pirate

This pirate is using a telescope to spy on her enemies and make sure nobody reaches the treasure before her.

## Pirate

Some pirates carry swords but this one has a gun. His hat has three corners and is called a tricorn.

## Governor

The Governor is in charge of the Navy. The navy's job is to stop pirates from stealing treasure.

## Soldier

The Navy's soldiers sail the seven seas trying to prevent any crime being caused by pirates.

## King Kuahka

The chief of the Islanders wears a large headdress. He lives on a desert island that hides some valuable treasure.

## Skeleton

Spooky skeletons also roam the seven seas. Watch out!

# LEGO® SPACE

Astronauts travel in amazing spaceships to explore planet Mars, sometimes meeting aliens along the way. When necessary, the space police step in to fight criminal aliens from the Black Hole Gang.

## Astronaut
The LEGO® spacemen fly huge shuttles to outer space. Sometimes they need to defend themselves against aliens.

## Alien Commander
The alien commander pilots the Alien Infiltrator spaceship. The aliens on Mars are green and some glow in the dark!

## Insectoid
The insectoids are a group of aliens that look like insects. They drive amazing vehicles, such as the Bi-Wing Blaster and the Arachnoid Star Base.

## Mini-Robot
This mini-robot lives on Mars to help the Mars Mission astronauts. He carries a pick and a gun.

## Space Policeman

The space police protect the humans from alien criminals such as Squidman, Kranxx, Frenzy, Snake, The Skull Twins, and Slizer.

## Space Policeman and Skull Twin 1

This space policeman has caught an alien criminal red-handed. The criminal is one of the Skull Twins.

## Slizer

Slizer is an alien criminal from the Black Hole Gang that the Space Policemen are trying to catch.

## Squidman

Squidman is an alien criminal who has committed burglaries and vandalism. He also once broke a fellow criminal called Snake out of jail.

## Snake

Snake is an alien criminal. He has six eyes on his head and one on his stomach.

# LEGO® ADVENTURERS

Johnny Thunder is on a mission. He travels with his uncle Dr. Kilroy, and girlfriend Pippin Reed to far away places. They have been on adventures to Egypt, the jungle, Dino Island, and the Far East!

## Johnny Thunder

This brave Australian explorer is prepared for anything. He never gets scared.

## Pippin Reed

Journalist Pippin Reed accompanies Johnny Thunder on his adventures.

## Dr. Kilroy

Johnny's uncle shares many of his adventures and acts as a father figure to the explorer. He always wears his trademark pith helmet.

## Pharoah Hotep

Johnny Thunder met Pharoah Hotep on a mission to Egypt.

## Achu

Achu is guardian of the ancient treasures. He tries to stop Johnny Thunder and Señor Palomar from getting the sun disc.

## Baron Von Barron

This former army general is one of the world's most wanted men. He collects gemstones as a hobby.

## Señor Palomar

Johnny Thunder meets Señor Palomar in the jungle. He is head of a crime group which steals gems.

## Maharaja Lallu

The Maharaja is a greedy and selfish tyrant. He joins forces with Lord Sinister to search for the treasure of the Scorpion Palace.

## Emperor Chang Wu

This evil emperor lives at the Dragon Fortress. Johnny Thunder comes up against him on his expedition to the Orient.

## Ngan Pa

Ngan Pa is a corrupt Yeti hunter who Johnny Thunder meets while he is exploring in the Orient.

## Lord Sam Sinister

Lord Sam Sinister changed his name from Mr. Hates. He is always very smartly dressed.

# LEGO® AGENTS

Secret agents are trying to save mankind from evil plots. The agents wear jetpacks, drive fast cars, and ride on speedboats. It can be a glamorous life, but also a dangerous one!

## Agent Fuse

Agent fuse has been involved in the most missions. He has traveled to volcanoes, along rivers and hunted for gold in a jet plane.

## Agent Charge

Agent Charge is in the Aerial Defence Unit. In the past he has worked in a swamp and on a deep sea quest.

## Agent Chase

The leader of the agents is Agent Chase. He is involved in the most dangerous missions. He usually wears sunglasses.

TGD-2000

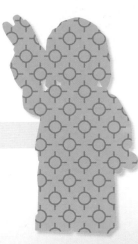

## Dr. Inferno

Dr. Inferno is the arch-enemy of the agents. He uses henchmen to help him carry out his evil plans. He was once captured by the agents but broke free.

## Agent Trace

Agent Trace was the only female agent in the team until an agent called Swift joined them.

## Agent Swipe

Agent Swipe was involved in a motorcycle chase to catch thief Gold Tooth when he stole a statue.

## Dyna-Mite

Dyna-Mite is another of Dr. Inferno's henchmen. She fought Agent Fuse on a big boat during a river heist.

## Slime Face

Slime Face is one of Dr. Inferno's henchmen who has been genetically altered. His face is always covered in slime.

## Fire Arm

Fire Arm is one of Dr. Inferno's helpers. He is a cyborg like Spy Clops. He has a cannon instead of a right arm.

## Spy Clops

This henchman has four eyes and eight legs which makes him look like a giant claw!

## Dr. D. Zaster

Dr. D. Zaster is an old friend of Dr. Inferno, who plans to slime LEGO® city. His plot is foiled by Agent Chase.

# LEGO® EXO-FORCE™

At the base of the Sentai montains, humans and robots are competing for supremacy. The EXO-FORCE team has many battle vehicles, but the robots will do anything in their quest to win. Deep in the jungle, the war rages on.

## Hikaru

Hikaru started out in the EXO-FORCE team as a test driver for all their new machines. He is now a top pilot and an amazing fighter.

## Sensei Keiken

The leader of the EXO-FORCE team, Sensei Keiken, is a wise man. He built the first battle machine and also the first enemy robot!

## Hitomi

Hitomi is the only female member of the EXO-FORCE team. She is a mechanic, but prefers to be doing martial arts and dreaming about being a pilot.

## Ryo

The EXO-FORCE team's technical expert designed the battle machines. He knows how to fix anything!

## Takeshi

Takeshi is a very powerful and focused man. He can be very aggressive but directs that towards the enemy robots!

## Ha-ya-to

This member of the team is a risk-taker with a sense of humor. He is an amazing pilot too, so an asset to the EXO-FORCE team.

## Iron Drone

The Iron Drone robot is a tough enemy. It never gives up and leaves a trail of destruction in its path.

## Devastator

The Devastator is a cunning robot who likes to think up sneaky plans to defeat the EXO-FORCE team.

## Meca One

Meca One is the leader of the robots and was the first to rise up against the humans. There is also a clone of this determined robot.

# UNDERGROUND

Deep underground, the power miners are looking for energy crystals. They have to get crystals, which they mine with special vehicles. They also battle with rock monsters!

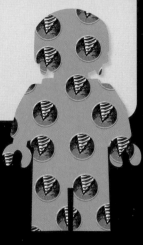

### Axel
Axel is a rock raider. He is an expert on all vehicles and is at his happiest when driving the Chrome Crusher.

### Chief
The chief is the oldest, wisest, and most experienced rock raider. He has one artificial arm after an accident on Pluto.

### Sparks
Sparks is one of the rock raiders' engineers, but he is very clumsy.

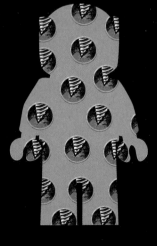

### Jet
Jet is a courageous and talented pilot. She is very stubborn and likes to get her own way.

### Power Miner
The power miners wear blue overalls and use pickaxes and thunder drillers to mine crystals from under the ground.

## Boulderax

Boulderax is strong, slow, and dumb. This rock monster will fight just for the fun of it.

## Power Miner

This power miner has found a crystal and takes it away so the rock monsters can't get to it.

## Meltrox

Meltrox is another rock monster. He is angry and destructive and hates everyone and everything.

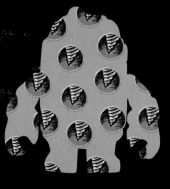

# LEGO® AQUARAIDERS

Aquanauts fight mutant sea creatures and stingray in the pursuit of deep sea treasure. In their quest for valuable coins, crystals, and jewels, they use lots of special equipment and must be fearless!

### Aqua Raider Diver

The aqua raiders use very powerful equipment for their underwater explorations. They use fast vehicles, strong drills and deadly weapons.

### Aqua Raider Diver

Aqua raiders need special equipment for their ocean explorations. They need breathing apparatus, flippers, and goggles.

### Aqua Raider Diver

The raiders have spear guns to keep dangerous sharks at bay. Some of their vehicles also have harpoon guns on them.

### Aqua Raider Diver

The aqua raiders find amazing jewels and treasure inside shipwrecks.

### Aqua Raider Diver

The divers use powerful drills to uncover treasure deep in the ocean floor.

## Aqua Raider Diver

Fast sea scooters help the divers reach treasure without meeting too many scary sea creatures!

## Aqua Raider Diver

The aqua raiders wear black helmets with a blue trident on the top. A trident is a three-pronged spear used for fishing.

## Aqua Raider Diver

The divers need flippers to help them swim fast under water. Sometimes they need to out-swim giant squid, giant crabs, or sharks.

## Aqua Raider Diver

The divers sometimes find large chests filled with jewels on the bottom of the ocean. They must drag them back to the base before sharks arrive!

## Skeleton King

The aqua raiders find a skeleton king in a shipwreck. He is still guarding his treasure of gold coins and jewels.

# LEGO® BATMAN™

Bruce Wayne is secretly a superhero. As the caped crusader Batman, he defends Gotham City from several different baddies and is aided by his reliable sidekick, Robin.

## Batman™

Bruce Wayne uses his wealth and intelligence to fight all the different bad guys of Gotham City. His costume makes him look like a bat!

## Robin

Batman's sidekick is always loyal. He wears a colorful costume and a green mask.

## Bruce Wayne

When he is not fighting crime, Batman is Bruce Wayne Bruce is a very rich businessman.

## Catwoman™

One of Batman's many enemies is Catwoman. She wears a mask like a cat and mainly carries out burglaries.

## Harley Quinn™

This villain dresses in a harlequin costume. She knows the Joker from Arkham Asylum where she used to work.

## The Joker™

The Joker is Batman's arch enemy. He will stop at nothing to win out against the caped superhero!

## The Penguin™

The Penguin is a gangster who acts like a gentleman. He loves birds and unusual umbrellas.

## The Riddler™

The Riddler is obsessed with riddles and puzzles and uses them to leave clues for the police and Batman about his latest crimes.

## Two Face™

Harvey Dent was a lawyer. He had an accident that left half his face scarred and turned to crime, renaming himself Two Face.

## Scarecrow™

This baddie dresses like a scarecrow. He enjoys scaring the residents of Gotham City but luckily Batman is there to save them.

## Mr. Freeze™

He used to be a scientist but an accident meant Mr. Freeze can only survive in very cold temperatures. His gun can freeze people.

# LEGO® ATLANTIS

Deep in the ocean lies the legendary city of Atlantis. Professor Sam Rhodes has found a map that may lead to the lost city. A submarine transports explorers to find the city and dodge weird and wonderful sea creatures.

## Axel Storm

Axel Storm is the technical expert of the Atlantis Deep Sea Salvage Crew. He is very serious and doesn't have time to joke. He has machines to fix!

## Captain Ace Speedman

Ace Speedman is the captain of the Neptune submarine that is taking the Atlantis Deep Sea Salvage Crew to the remains of the lost city of Atlantis.

## Bobby Buoy

Bobby Buoy is the apprentice of the group. He is young and inexperienced but he is always keen to help out—even if he does make a lot of mistakes!

## Dr. Jeff Fisher

Dr. Jeff Fisher is the marine biologist of the Crew. He is funny and friendly but also very clumsy. His dream is to discover a new species of sea life.

## Lance Spears

Lance Spears is the First Mate in the Atlantis Deep Sea Salvage Crew. He loves deep sea diving but he is easily scared by the sea creatures.

## Professor Sam Rhodes

Professor Sam Rhodes is very intelligent. She often makes jokes that the rest of the Crew don't understand!

## Squid Warrior

The Squid Warrior lives in Squid Temple. He is half-man and half-squid and can be very aggressive. Sometimes he trips himself up on his own tenticles and he inks himself when he is surprised.

## Shark Warrior

The Shark Warrior lives in Shark Castle. He has the head of a shark and the body of a human. He is always thinking about food!

## Manta Warrior

The Manta Warrior has the body of a human and the head of a manta ray. He lives on the large seaweed bed and he likes to chase his own tail.

# LEGO® *STAR WARS*™

In a galaxy far, far away lie many strange planets and even stranger creatures. The Rebel Alliance battles throughout the galaxy to restore the ideals of the Old Republic. The Jedi must put the Force and their lightsabers to good use.

### Anakin Skywalker™

Anakin is Luke Skywalker's father. He serves the Galactic Republic but then goes on to become the evil Darth Vader!

### Princess Leia™

Leia is the daughter of Anakin and twin sister of Luke. She has a strong and intelligent character. She is famous for her leadership during the Galactic Civil War.

### Yoda™

Yoda is the most powerful and wise of the Jedi masters. He trains Obi-Wan Kenobi and nearly all the other Jedi in the Order.

### R2-D2™

R2-D2 is an Astromech Droid who serves the Skywalker family for years. He is very bold and brave.

### Obi-Wan Kenobi™

This legendary Jedi master is a member of the Jedi High Council. Obi-Wan Kenobi is quiet and calm but has amazing lightsaber skills!

### Jabba the Hutt™

Jabba is one of the most famous Hutt crime lords in the galaxy. He is Han Solo's arch enemy.

## Jango Fett™

Jango Fett is a bounty hunter who works for Count Dooku. He has a son called Boba who is a clone.

## C-3PO™

This cautious protocol droid loyally serves over 40 masters. He is a friend of R2-D2 and they are often seen together.

## Han Solo™

Han Solo is a human. He is a member of the Rebel Alliance and the New Republic. He pilots the *Millennium Falcon*™ and helps to destroy the Death Star!

## Battle Droid Commander

The Battle Droid Commander leads the battle droids. He usually carries a gun.

## Luke Skywalker™

Luke helps to defeat the Galactic Empire and found the New Republic. He fights in many important battles.

## Darth Vader™

Anakin Skywalker's anger leads him to the dark side and he becomes Darth Vader, master of the dark side. He is enemy to all the Jedi.

## Chewbacca™

Chewbacca is a Wookiee and also the co-pilot of Han Solo's *Millennium Falcon*™. He is very wise and loyal.

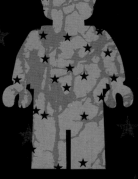

# LEGO® HARRY POTTER™

Schoolboy wizard Harry Potter spends many of his schooldays at Hogwarts fighting the evil force of Lord Voldemort. Harry has some close schoolmates, but not everyone at Hogwarts is on his side.

### Harry Potter™

Harry is the most famous wizard at Hogwarts. He is a prefect in Gryffindor house and is captain of the quidditch team. And he still finds time to fight evil!

### Ron Weasley™

Ron is in Gryffindor with Harry and Hermione and he plays Keeper on the Quidditch team. He helped to keep the Philosopher's Stone from Quirrell.

### Hermione Granger™

Hermione is best friends with Harry and Ron. She is a prefect and a model student. She is really good at most things!

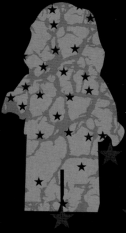

### Draco Malfoy™

A prefect of Slytherin house, Draco Malfoy is Harry Potter's arch enemy at Hogwarts. His father is Death Eater Lucius Malfoy.

### Professor Dumbledore™

The headmaster of Hogwarts is also the greatest wizard in the world. He is the only wizard that Voldemort fears.

### Hagrid™

Hagrid is the gamekeeper at Hogwarts school. He supports Dumbledore and is friends with Harry. He is also half-human and half-giant.

## Lord Voldemort™

Born Tom Riddle, he grew up in a muggle orphanage. He later became the best Dark Wizard in the world and changed his name to Voldemort.

## Professor Snape™

Severus Snape is a teacher at Hogwarts School of Witchcraft and Wizardry. When he was younger, he was a talented wizard who specialized in the Dark Arts.

## Death Eater™

The Death Eaters are Lord Voldemort's helpers. They wear black hoods and sometimes only reveal their eyes.

## Professor Dolores Umbridge™

She may look sweet, but Dolores Umbridge is hungry for power. She is now in Askaban jail for her crimes against Muggle-borns.

HOGWARTS EXPRESS™

5972

# LEGO® INDIANA JONES™

Indiana Jones™ is an intrepid explorer. He travels to deserts and jungles in search of ancient artefacts. Sometimes he has to race to get to a valuable artefact before it is stolen by somebody else!

### Henry Jones Snr.

Indiana Jones's father, Henry, is also a talented archaeologist. He introduced his son to adventure and also the quest for the Holy Grail.

### Indiana Jones™

Indiana Jones arms himself with a whip and a gun as he roams the world. He is looking for famous artefacts such as the Holy Grail and the Ark of the Covenant.

### René Belloq

Rene Belloq is Indy's rival. He is looking for the same artefacts, but wants to keep them for himself. Indiana Jones gives them to museums.

### Marion Ravenwood

Marion helps Indiana Jones with his explorations. Her father was a famous archaeologist too.

## Mola Ram

Mola Ram is one of Indiana Jones's enemies. He is high priest of the scary Thuggee cult in India.

## Akator Skeleton

This skeleton is from the ancient city of Akator. The city was made from gold in the Amazonian rainforest.

## Ugha Warrior

This warrior is from the Ugha tribe which lives deep in the jungle in South America.

## Cairo Henchman

Indiana and Marion have to try and escape this henchman in Cairo, Egypt. There there are many ancient artefacts in Egypt.

# LEGO® SPONGEBOB SQUAREPANTS™

Down in Bikini Bottom, in the middle of the Pacific Ocean, lives a little sea sponge called SpongeBob SquarePants™. He is a chef at the Krusty Krab, the most popular restaurant in Bikini Bottom.

## SpongeBob SquarePants™

SpongeBob is a popular sponge. He is also a great cook and not bad at karate. He could definitely improve his driving, though!

## Patrick Star

SpongeBob's best friend Patrick is always having hair-brained ideas. Things don't always go to plan when Patrick is involved!

## Sandy Cheeks Astronaut

Sandy is a land squirrel who has a love-hate relationship with SpongeBob SquarePants.

## Mr. Krabs

Mr. Krabs is a descendent of King Krabs. He owns the fast food restaurant where SpongeBob works.

## Squidward Tentacles

Squidward is actually an octopus. He also changes color as often as he changes his mood!

## Plankton

He may be small, but Plankton is very smart and cunning. He is often underestimated by naive SpongeBob.

## Mrs. Puff

Mrs. Puff is a driving teacher. She gets in all kinds of trouble when she tries to teach SpongeBob to drive!